# Anne Frank

## The Girl Heard Around The World

By Linda Elovitz Marshall
Illustrations by Aura Lewis

Orchard Books • New York
An Imprint of Scholastic Inc.

All her life, Anne Frank wanted to be heard.

Really, truly heard.

As a baby, Anne cried. LOUD.
As a toddler, she was silly and made everyone laugh.
And as a little girl, she spoke her mind.

But sometimes no one listened.
Some things were hard to talk about.
And, sometimes, it seemed like no one understood.

Anne was born on June 12, 1929, in Frankfurt, Germany. Her family, like many other Jewish families, had lived in Germany for centuries. But a few years after Anne was born, life there changed. A man named Adolf Hitler came into power and took over the government. Hitler and his followers, the Nazis, blamed the Jews for the country's problems.

Everyone who was Jewish, including Anne and her family, was in danger.

Translation: "Jews are unwanted here."

Anne was four when her family left Germany in search of safety. They moved to Amsterdam, the capital city of a neighboring country called the Netherlands.

There Anne learned to speak Dutch,
to ride a bike,
and to read and write.

Anne liked making mischief.
From the balcony of her second-floor apartment,
she occasionally sprinkled water on people walking below.
In school, she talked and talked.
She especially liked telling jokes and riddles.

Translation: "Jewish Quarter" (top line: German, bottom line: Dutch).

But in 1940, when Anne was 11, Hitler and the Nazis took over the Netherlands, too. Life for Jews became just as dangerous there as it was in Germany. The Nazis enforced strict rules on all Jews. No one was allowed to speak out against the Nazis. Anyone who spoke out could be arrested and killed.

JUDEN VIERTEL
JOODSCHE WIJK

And yet, Anne needed
to talk to someone.

She needed to be heard . . .
really, truly heard.

On her 13th birthday Anne received a gift —
a red plaid diary, with a lock and key!
Anne named her diary "Kitty."

Anne wrote to Kitty about everything.
She shared her feelings, her thoughts,
the things buried deep in her heart.

She wrote about new rules that stopped
her — and all Jews — from

    riding bikes,
    going to movies,
    playing in public parks,
    and attending public school . . .

    New rules that made her wear a
    Star of David on her clothing.

Translation of "Jood": Jew

Anne wrote about being called a "chatterbox" by her teacher in her all-Jewish school,

about a poem she wrote *about* chatterboxes, and how the poem won her teacher's praise.

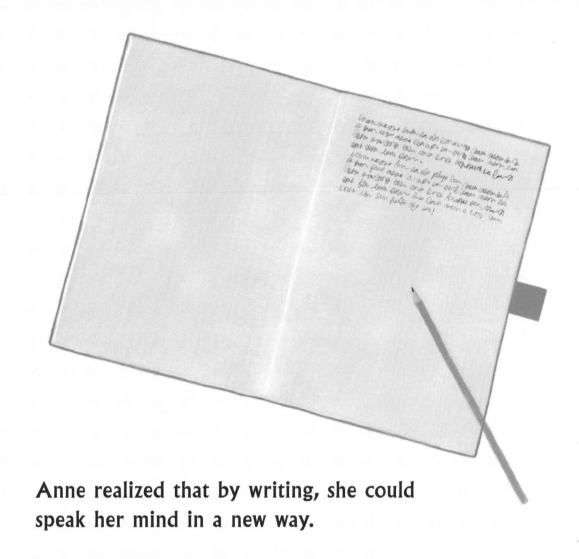

Anne realized that by writing, she could
speak her mind in a new way.

She could really, truly be heard.

One morning in 1942, just a few weeks after her 13th birthday, Anne's mother woke her very early. It was time to flee. It had become too dangerous to be Jewish in Amsterdam. Anne and her family were going into hiding.

Anne put on all the clothes she could. She gathered her most treasured things. She packed her diary first.

Anne, her sister, mother, and father moved into a
secret annex in the back of a warehouse. The warehouse
was part of the business her father had once owned.
Four other people went into hiding with them.

All were Jewish, all in need of a safe place.

Only a few trusted, non-Jewish friends knew where
Anne and the others went. These friends still worked in
the warehouse, making it easier for them to deliver food
and supplies.

In hiding, Anne tried to continue her normal life. She decorated a wall with movie star photos. She kept up with her studies, and she read and read and *read*.

But life in hiding was difficult and lonely.

During the day, everyone in hiding had to tiptoe and whisper. If the workers in the warehouse below discovered them, Anne and the others could be arrested. An arrest would mean prison . . . or worse.

Instead of telling jokes, chattering with friends, and making mischief, Anne became quiet. Sometimes, she was VERY quiet.

But Anne couldn't stay quiet for long.
Now Anne wrote about her life in hiding.
She told it all.
She wrote what she could not say.

She wrote about birthdays and holidays,
about missing her friends,
about wishing she could hear birds sing.

She wrote about giving her father a haircut,
about playing with the warehouse cat,
about gazing out the attic window,
looking at people below.

Anne wrote about longing for nature, sunlight, and freedom.

She wrote about being afraid,
about hearing bombings from the skies above.

She wrote about wishing people could live together

When the closeness got too much, eight people together,
always together . . .
    day after day *after day*, Anne wrote.

Anne spoke her mind to Kitty . . .
    who was *always* there to listen,
        always there to understand.

When Anne argued with her mother
   or felt jealous of her sister,
   when she thought she was about to cry . . .
      Anne wrote what she could not say.

When Anne got angry —
   because someone wanted to read her diary,
   or scolded her for saying the wrong thing —
      Anne wrote what she could not say.

Unable to go outside, Anne imagined and wrote
stories about
      a teddy bear off to see the world,
      a good fairy who made people happy,
      a kindly grandmother who became her
      granddaughter's guardian angel.

When water spilled, soaking her work,
Anne, heartsick and almost in tears, rushed
to rescue her pages. She would not let her
words be drowned.

For two years in hiding, Anne wrote what she
could not speak. She hoped that when the war
was over, she might publish a book about life
in the secret annex.

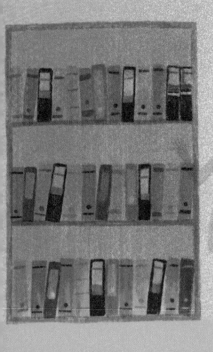

But on August 4, 1944, Nazi police discovered the secret hiding place. Anne, her family, and their friends were captured and arrested. They were taken away to prisons . . . and worse. After the Nazi police left, a friend who had helped Anne and the others gathered Anne's diary and writings. She kept them safe, hoping that when the war was over she could return them to Anne.

Anne died in the winter of 1945, just weeks before the war ended. Of the eight Jews in hiding, only her father survived.

After the war ended, that friend gave the diary and writings to Anne's father. He published them in a book known around the world as *Anne Frank: The Diary of a Young Girl.* Since then, Anne's writings and her diary have been translated into 70 languages.

The war had tried to silence her,
but Anne told it all.

She wrote what she could not say . . .

*And the whole world heard!*

# Anne Frank: The Girl Heard Around the World

Anne Frank was born on June 12, 1929, in Frankfurt, Germany. She was the younger of Otto and Edith Frank's two children and part of a Jewish family that had lived in Germany for generations. When Hitler and the Nazis took over Germany in 1933, all Jews throughout Germany were in danger. Others were in danger, too, including gay people, the Romani people (Roma), people with disabilities, Jehovah's Witnesses, Afro-Germans, and political dissidents. Seeking safety, Anne and her family left their homeland to settle in the Netherlands in 1934. But Hitler's troops were on the move. Hitler's troops took over Poland in 1939, then the Netherlands in 1940. Hitler and the Nazis planned to kill all Jews in Europe, including Anne. Fearing for their lives, the Frank family and four other people, all Jewish — the Van Pels family and Fritz Pfeffer — went into hiding. While in hiding, Anne poured her feelings into her diary. She wrote what she could not say. She hoped that the war would soon end and that she would be free. That didn't happen. On August 4, 1944, their hiding place was discovered. All of the people in hiding in the secret annex were arrested, imprisoned, and sent to Nazi concentration camps. Anne and her sister, Margot, died in February or March 1945. The exact date is not known. Five of the others, including Anne's mother, were gassed to death or died of illness. The only survivor was Anne's father, Otto Frank. After the war, he received Anne's diary from Miep Gies, one of the trusted non-Jewish helpers who had sustained the eight people in hiding and who, after the arrest, gathered Anne's diary and writings and hid them from the Nazis. Anne's diary, first published in 1947, is among the world's most-read books, translated into 70 languages, with more than 30 million copies sold.

# Timeline

**May 8, 1925** — Anne's parents, Otto Frank and Edith Holländer, are married.

**July 18, 1925** — Publication of Adolf Hitler's book *Mein Kampf*.

**February 16, 1926** — Anne's sister, Margot, is born.

**June 12, 1929** — Anne is born.

**October 29, 1929** — Stock markets crash, worldwide, sending many countries into an economic depression. In the US, the Great Depression begins.

**January 30, 1933** — Adolf Hitler appointed chancellor of Germany.

**April 1, 1933** — Hitler's Nazi party prohibits German citizens from patronizing Jewish shops, doctors, and lawyers.

**July 4, 1933** — Otto Frank sets up his company, Opekta, in Amsterdam, Netherlands.

**July 14, 1933** — Germany bans political parties other than the Nazi party, destroying democracy and creating a dictatorship. Hitler and the Nazis are in total control. Anyone publicly opposing them faces dire consequences.

**December 1933–February 1934** — Anne, Margot, and their mother move to Amsterdam. Shortly afterward, Anne's Dutch schooling begins.

**September 1935** — In Germany, "Race Laws" strip Jews of rights. Among other restrictions marriage between Jews and non-Jews becomes illegal.

**November 9, 1938** — "Kristallnacht" — Nazis destroy synagogues, Jewish businesses and homes throughout Germany and Austria.

**September 1, 1939** — Germany invades Poland. In response, Britain and France declare war on Germany.

**May 10, 1940** — Germany attacks and occupies the Netherlands.

**October 1941** — Jewish children in the Netherlands are prohibited from attending regular public schools and are restricted to Jewish-only schools.

**December 7, 1941** — Japan bombs Pearl Harbor. As a result, the US declares war on Japan. Germany then sides with Japan and declares war on the US.

**January 20, 1942** — In Berlin, Nazi officials plan "The Final Solution" — the murder of Europe's 11 million Jews.

**May 3, 1942** — In the Netherlands, Jews over the age of six must wear the Star of David on their clothing to designate them as Jews.

**June 12, 1942** — Anne's 13th birthday. She receives a plaid diary with a lock and key.

**July 5, 1942** — Margot receives notice (a "call-up") to report for "work" in Germany. Anne's family is aware that others who have been "called up" never return.

**July 6, 1942** — In haste, the Frank family goes into hiding in the secret annex at 263 Prinsengracht, Amsterdam. Later they are joined by the Van Pels family and Fritz Pfeffer.

**June 6, 1944** — **D-Day** — Allied troops land in France.

**August 4, 1944** — Nazi Gestapos (German secret state police) raid the annex, arresting and imprisoning the Frank family and their friends.

**August 8, 1944** — Anne and the others are sent to the Westerbork Transit Camp in the Netherlands to await deportation to the killing centers.

**September 3, 1944** — Anne and the others are sent to Auschwitz-Birkenau, a large Nazi killing center in Poland.

October–November 1944 — Anne and Margot are transferred to another Nazi concentration camp in Germany, Bergen-Belsen.

January 6, 1945 — Edith Frank dies in Auschwitz.

January 27, 1945 — The Russian army liberates Auschwitz.

February or March 1945 (exact date is uncertain) — Weak from starvation and unsanitary conditions, both Anne and Margot die of typhus in the Bergen-Belsen concentration camp. Anne is 16 years old.

May 8, 1945 — V-E Day — The Nazis are defeated. Europe is liberated.

June 3, 1945 — Otto Frank, the only survivor of the annex, returns to Amsterdam.

July 18, 1945 — Otto receives Anne's diary and learns that Anne and Margot have died.

June 25, 1947 — Anne's diary is published in the Netherlands.

# Author's Note

As a third-generation American Jew raised in suburban Boston shortly after World War II, I was shielded from the horrors of the Nazis, Hitler, and antisemitism. I'd overheard talk, but only in hushed tones.

For example, I remember a boy around the corner from me who had a pogo stick and stilts, such wonderful toys that I envied him. But when I asked about his toys, I was told — in hushed tones — that his parents had been in *the camps. Don't ask anything else* was the message. *It's too painful to talk about.* Then, when I was in fifth grade, my Hebrew school teacher, a frail man in his late 50s with deep bags under his eyes, told our class that he'd been a partisan, had fought in the Resistance, and had been imprisoned in a Nazi concentration camp. Numbers were tattooed on his forearm.

That teacher, Mr. Carl Cohen, suggested we read *The Diary of Anne Frank*. Moved and inspired by Anne's writings, I began keeping my own diary. Years later, when Mr. Cohen — who was a part-time Harvard mathematics professor as well as a Hebrew teacher — was once again my teacher, he introduced me to his wife, to literature, to philosophy, and to America's fight for civil rights. Like many good teachers, he also became a good friend. It is partly for him that my youngest daughter is named.

And it is for him, for the six million Jews, for all those murdered in the Holocaust, and for all humanity that I share Anne's story. In the words of the historian Simon Dubnow, "Write, Jews, write it down!" Tell your children. Never forget.

## Partial List of Sources

Frank, Anne. *Anne Frank: The Diary of a Young Girl*, translated from the Dutch by B. M. Mooyaart-Doubleday. New York: Bantam Books, 1993.

Frank, Anne. *Anne Frank's Tales from the Secret Annex*, edited by Gerrold Van Der Stroom and Susan Massotty, translated by Susan Massotty. New York: Bantam Books, 2003.

Jacobson, Sid, and Ernie Colón. *Anne Frank: The Anne Frank House Authorized Graphic Biography*. Hill and Wang, a division of Farrar, Straus, and Giroux, 2015.

Müller, Melissa. *Anne Frank: The Biography*. New York: Picador, 2014.

## Suggestions for Further Reading

Abramson, Ann. *Who Was Anne Frank?* New York: Grossett & Dunlap, 2007.

Pincus, Meeg. *Miep and the Most Famous Diary: The Woman Who Rescued Anne Frank's Diary*. Sleeping Bear Press, Ann Arbor, MI, 2019.

## Websites

The United States Holocaust Memorial Museum, https://www.ushmm.org

The Anne Frank House, https://www.annefrank.org/en/

To my children and grandchildren . . . that they may live free of antisemitism and other injustices — and to the memory and honor of Holocaust survivors dear to me, my family, and friends: Gertie Boyarski, Carl Cohen, Sidney and Libby Glucksman, and Miriam London (known to all who loved her as Baba), and to the millions murdered because they were Jews, because they were different.
— L.E.M.

For my parents, Susan and Yedidya Fraiman, with love.
— A.L.

Library of Congress Cataloging-in-Publication Data Available
ISBN 978-1-338-31229-4 • 10 9 8 7 6 5 4 3 2 1   20 21 22 23 24 • Printed in Malaysia   108
First edition, September 2020
Aura Lewis's illustrations were rendered digitally. The book was typeset in Albertus, which was designed by Berthold Wolpe in 1932. Book design by Brian LaRossa.